# NATURAL PHILOSOPHIES

By the same author

Voluntary (2020)

By the same author:

*Chronicity* (2020)

# NATURAL PHILOSOPHIES

# MICHAEL J. LEACH

RECENT
WORK
PRESS

Natural Philosophies
Recent Work Press
Canberra, Australia

Copyright © Michael J. Leach, 2022

ISBN: 9780645180855 (paperback)

A catalogue record for this
book is available from the
National Library of Australia

Cover image: *Blue Mountains, New South Wales, Australia* (2019)  by Quentin
Grignet via unsplash
Cover design: Recent Work Press
Set by Recent Work Press

recentworkpress.com

ss

*For Rachel and my family*

# Contents

# PART ONE
# PLANETARIUM

# This Place of Birth

*Dja Dja Wurrung Country, May-June 2021*

i.
the sovereignty
of this grey-gold land—
                    never ceded

ii.
nature
reserve—
magpies & kookaburras

                                        flutter & cry

iii.
                    day 1 of lock
-down 4.0—
i kneel in soil to change
a flat tyre

iv.
one year since Mum was
                    buried neath gumtrees—
i can't go back
or move on

# Constellations

of uniquely spaced,

silvery stars

burn hydrogen

through aeons

to illuminate the depths

of space

and time,                              even though each light

is finite.          Behold the most marvellous

self-sacrifice

in the Universe.

# Eight Minutes, 20 Seconds, and an Instant

Scientists maintain
        it takes just
                eight minutes,
                      20 seconds
for invisible cosmic travellers     to depart an ever-burning orb,
                          traverse 150 million km of space,
                          filter through five layers of gases,
                          and reach an ever-orbiting orb.


Scientists also maintain that,       upon arrival,

the cosmic travellers instantly     absorb into exposed objects,
                          bounce off every surface,
                          refract through curved lenses,
                          and enter ever-gazing orbs.


In that same instant,            among other things,

the welcome travellers also       heat half a world of water,
                          paint landscapes and cityscapes,
                          change the phases of matter,
                          fabricate the hands of time,
                          energise solar panels and flora,
                          produce multicoloured spectra,
                          warm an enormous atmosphere,
                          refract through panes of glass,
                          illuminate stained-glass stories,
                          and heat half a world of lifeblood.
                            20 seconds, and  an instant.
                    eight minutes,
            pass in just
All this comes to

# This Contemporary Palette

*The purest and most thoughtful minds are those which love colour the most.*
> —John Ruskin, The Stones of Venice, *1851-1853*

The postmodern gothic absorbs like vantablack.
Our Universe's hue—cosmic latte—is a shade of beige.
These new age fashions shimmer in neo mint.
That red splattered on LED screens is dragon's blood.
Artists keep painting cerulean skies electric blue
while we turn to our dying Sun like heliotropes.

Our colour of mourning is heliotrope—
that age-old alternative to vantablack.
As our workplaces crackle with electric blue,
we tire of interiors that whisper in beige.
As our bloodshot eyes drink dragon's blood,
our home interiors shimmer in neo mint.

Your colour of the future is neo mint—
a green that honours plants like heliotrope
and *Dracaena* (the true source of dragon's blood).
All dimensions vanish in vantablack
yet reappear in familiar shades of beige.
My colour of the future is electric blue.

Lightning bolts colour our skies electric blue.
Pot plants brighten our offices with neo mint.
You ask, 'Who'd want to be as boring as beige
when you can be as quirky as heliotrope?'
We watch the Night's Watch vanish in vantablack
and the last Targaryens bleed dragon's blood.

I ask, 'Who'd believe dragons gave dragon's blood
in a world where science shines in electric blue?'
Scientists made VANTAs to create vantablack
and melded tech with nature to yield neo mint.
Your aura is a purple flower—heliotrope—
that stood out against a background of beige.

We painted our first home's walls beige
then exposed bricks the colour of dragon's blood.
We slow danced after planting those heliotropes.
I stumbled through a karaoke version of 'Electric Blue'
decades before lexicons swelled with colours like neo mint
and that darkest of shades—vantablack.

But now, in our beige Universe amidst the vantablack,
I recreate yellows from neo mint and dragon's blood
while you swirl violets from electric blue and heliotrope.

# Bioluminescence

I swim out to sea
and tread choppy waters
lit by the light of our resident star.

Before a rip can pull me,
I swim back to the comfort of our summery beach
to lay supine upon warm sands
and hold grains that glitter like distant suns.

The dry sand on my palm blows away in the wind
that made the last wave crash into wet sand.

I arise to walk this coastline for hours
in search of something far less grainy,
in need of something so smooth so exquisite so pure
that it's both down-to-earth                  &                  transcendent.

In time, I find a pearly nautilus shell
that fills my aural canals with its eloquence.

A divine voice summons me back to the deep,
to waters that grow calmer & darker
with the fading
light of a long midsummer's day.

I swim out to sea
and tread tranquil waters
in which there's now an eye-catching bloom

of gracefully pulsating crystal jellies
that defy the gloom with their luminescence.

# Symbological Statement

IF
$\Sigma 1$
told me
$\sqrt{\infty} \neq \infty$,
THEN
i would
respectfully ?
this + try
(as nice as $\pi$)
to bridge the ÷
with $\Sigma$thing
relatively $\int$
to all things
mathematical,
with $\Sigma$thing
that the 2
of us could still
100% agree on
in these $\Delta \times$
post 1984:
2
+

2

=

4

IF

1 is

¬ speaking

illogically

OR

in metaphor.

# N of 1

I take a convenience sample
from the small sampling
frame at the party.
I sample one person—you.
We talk over ice water
before you take my hand
and lead me

                                    outside,
saying you have something to show me.
As my eyes study the symmetrical beauty
of your fire-lit face,
cerebral matter recognises patterns
and makes new discoveries:
a wrinkle here,

                        a scar there.
I consider reaching out to touch
your flushed cheek
but the moment has already evaporated,
transmuting into

the next one.
Suddenly, you are a body in motion.
I step back to observe
the physics of your physique
dancing through space and time,
cutting cleanly through free-floating atoms—
the elements of this country air
that we inhale.
Your wrists
twist
before me so dextrously
that you could be working bright magic.
I am transfixed by the show.

That aluminium
staff you brandish
twirls rapidly before me,
glowing warmly at each end
as flaming wicks give off photons
to a starry, moonless night.
My eyes cannot
keep up with
the light;

the ring of fire
that you twirl
with practiced ease
chases itself into infinity
and back again
while undulating like a Möbius strip.

The smell is
                            combustive,
the sound
                            aerodynamic,
the sight
                            hypnotic.

I close my eyes but still see your fire
twirling on the backs of my eyelids.
In this afterimage, I glimpse
a familiar face lit by flames.
I consider my sample size:
n = 1.

# Fractional

*After Mari B-Li Donni's digital photograph* Fractional *(2020)*

Each one of us
is elemental & fractional—

a constituent part
(or perhaps parts)

of Empedocles'
four
classical elements.

Some may ask
what part(s) we are.

The scientists may say

we are the water
that comprises
such high proportions
of our bodies.

The morticians may say

we are the earth
from whence we came
& into which
we will
return.

The athletes may say

we are the air
thru which we rush
& deeply breathe
all the way
to painted lines.

The artists may say          we are the fire(!)
                             that burns within
                             the ancient kilns
                             of our beings.

The philosophers may say     that the actual
                             human fraction
                             of Empedocles'
                             classical elements
                             is exactly
                             four
                             -fourths.

# (Un)real

sometimes
I can't believe the world
around us is real

that impossibly blue
sky is a perfectly made
gaseous space—so spacious
                    so coloured
                    so multilayered


so what?

so not
possible without (un)natural
philosophy


                    fluffy

                                        free


                                                            -form
all these                                   floating
                clouds



must be held up by something, some
invisible or metaphorical cord

call it magic
or theologic
or physics

or a mix
of the above

no matter
what, it's wonderful


Be-                                                    sky
    hold                                         -y
        geese                         cloud
        flying                    blue
            in            sky
                a      thru
                    V

how
can that be?

you tell us
but

why
do so few question
the depth of our perception?

we are taught how
then left

wondering
why

# Atmospheric

I'm finally free falling like I did as a kid in hazy daydreams. The far-flung Sun colours my descent through an outer layer of hydrogen & helium gases, spray painting everything amber. My suit's sensors sense that I'm right at the base of the Jovian stratosphere, at an altitude near the haze layer & underlying troposphere. I'm under ever increasing atmospheric pressure. I'm drawn down, down through never ending, swirling clouds by that irresistible pull of general gravity, knowing full well I'll never reach solid ground. I'm otherworldly, out of my elements: a natural extension of thought experiments. Colleagues see me as a free-falling foreign body. Colleagues see me as further proof of that ancient theory of relativity conceived by an Earth physicist—Albert—& compellingly confirmed by an Earth engineer and computer scientist—Katie.

# Radio-luminous

You are the centre
of this spacious Solar System—
a beatific so(u)l
shining perennially,
radiating countless photons
in high-dimensional directions.

You are the star
that's closest to me.
Your heavenly
                    body burns brightly
with a glittering
gold-green
tinge.

You are the Aurora
Australis swing dancing up a solar
storm at night through the same
southern skies, glowing gold
-green & blue-violet
here till such time
as you decide to go north.

You are the person
with the radiant Duchenne smile
and silvery sienna strands
who's sitting cross-legged before me—
the one whose warm presence

I don't want to leave.

# My Peace Lily

*Adelaide, 2011*

Three thin stems
shoot from lush leaves—
the only greenery
within the confines
of my city apartment.

Three spadices
shaped like morning stars
shine in bright yellow,
their spikes less sharp
than rose thorns.

Three delicate petals
curve upwards to nibs,
reflecting every colour
in their surrender
to peace.

# My Harlequin

                                                                He
                                                                sits
       on green             grass
      grazed upon      for fibre
    &the wearing      down of
   unremittingly     growing
     cylindrical incisors & cheek
       teeth. He has momentarily
        raised his wedge-shaped
distance.         head to watch me from a

The biomathematics of his black-and-white coat reflects the feathers
of the magpies warbling nearby—singing the unofficial Aussie theme tune
of the Magpie Harlequin Rabbit. As the Sunday sun shines warmly on his body,
he does not sweat from any pores but, rather, releases heat from the labyrinthine
network of blood vessels up in those raised, rose-tinged ears. His white whiskers
undulate as he chews his last mouthful of grass & rests in my back garden,
tail at the ready to distract predators or attract mates. This Harlequin Rabbit & I
share European ancestry: his genes came from France; mine from the UK &
Poland. Beasts like us brought destruction. Sometimes he's playful
& hops hoops round my ankles. Presently, he's imperfectly still.
  His muscly hind legs     & front legs plant paws
  in the grass, brimming    with approximately
    ten Joules         of potential
                energy.

# West-East

Luscious
blushing spider orchids
(*Caladenia lorea*)
spread leggy pink petals
on a Western Australian
sandplain.

Beautiful
kangaroo apples
(*Solanum aviculare*)
bear purple flowers & red-
orange fruit amidst this east coast
rainforest.

Bristling
red toothbrushes
(*Grevillea hookeriana*)
brush passers-by
in the depths of a dry
summer.

Flamboyant
firewheel trees
(*Stenocarpus sinuatus*)
boast scarlet spokes
in the heart of the humid
tropics.

Upstanding
scarlet banksias
(*Banksia coccinea*)
raise up squat, cylindrical
pincushions in a native
backyard.

Elegant
bleeding-heart trees
(*Homalanthus populifolius*)
warmly welcome weekend
visitors in a native
front yard.

Hardy
tubada plants
(*Melaleuca phoenicea*)
grow green-blue leaves & red-
purple bottlebrush flowers
beside this west coast
watercourse.

Hardy
burrawang plants
(*Macrozamia communis*)
grow green fern-like leaves
& cantaloupe-coloured, pineapple-
shaped cones amidst this east coast
rainforest.

Fiery
lemon-scented myrtle
responding to its
botanical name—*Darwinia
citriodora*—is just as lemony
and significantly more
taxonomic.

A rosy
Sydney rose
responding to its
botanical name—*Boronia
serrulata*—is just as sweet
and dramatically more
taxonomic.

The red-and-green kangaroo paw
(*Anigozanthos manglesii*)
is blossoming with long, curved
mammalian fingers, its morphology
singularly spectacular

The New South Wales waratah
(*Telopea speciosissima*)
is blossoming with a fluoro red
flower arrangement, its morphology
singularly spectacular

& emblematic.

# In Memory of an Island Species

*It's the animals that make us human.*
—*Leah Kaminsky,* The Hollow Bones *(2019)*

She had a given name
—Gump—
& a secluded home—
Christmas Island.
She was the last known
member of her species:
an individual

known to scientists & keepers
as both a friend & an endling.

She received close
attention & affection from humans
after losing her reptilian kin.
She was a lone

Christmas Island Forest Skink
(*Emoia

        nativitatis*).

It was Jan. 2014
when scientists put her on a list
of Australian threatened species,
classifying her kind as critically
endangered.

Humans combed the rainforests
coating Christmas Island's
135 km²
area

in search of a candidate mate
who was nowhere to be found.

Gump was found
lifeless
on the eve of winter
2014, only months
after her kind

was belatedly
listed as critically endangered.

She left us a legacy
& another
lesson.

# Vestiges of Natural History

to walk on soil the Sun dried.

concealing earth neath six feet.

conferred by trees spared from blades.

and head down a track of sorts.

then descends on worn footwear.

trees and feel refreshed yet glum.

that run at first and then fly

This landscape has been short-changed.

My dog and I step outside

We cross dead grass to concrete

We pass in and out of shade

We reach the curve of our court

The dirt ascends in hot air

I stand among reserved gum

My dog gives chase to magpies

over lands humans have changed.

# The Australian Anthropo-seen

Up there
in the gumtree,    we see    the unmistakable
symbol of the Australian bush—the humble koala
(*Phascolarctos cinereus*). Two huge round fluffy ears
make it easy to hear what is happening up high
& down low. Hazelnut eyes watch
while a large spoon-shaped nose
remains ready to determine the levels
of toxic molecules in any given eucalyptus
leaf. The humble koala is wholly dependent
on eucalyptus trees: its sole source of sustenance
& shelter. This arboreal marsupial is adaptable yet vulnerable to the effects
of global warming. The ever-increasing $CO_2$ levels in Earth's atmosphere
have begun to change the chemical composition of
eucalyptus leaves, raising concentrations of tannins
& reducing concentrations of proteins to the point
where nutritional value is compromised. Meanwhile, the flames
of Australia's increasingly intense bushfire seasons burn more
& more koalas & their gumtree homes.
These changes may be more than our
symbolic marsupial
can stand.

# Summer Air

*a renga written with Rachel Rayner*

A summer smog clouds
warm air, enshrouding landmarks.
Fog lights brighten streets.

Particles are so dark
they redden the Sun's glare

on cracked concrete paths
walked by breathers of smoke
blown in from the bush,

from the disintegrating
leaves & the combusting bark.

Erupting infernos
of hot colours roar, feeding
on lives & homes

that spark and collapse into
voids, scorched with loss.

Winged seeds rise
from within flaming gum trees
to fly through thick air

and soon land on damp soils
where life grows, greening, skyward.

# Keeper

|        |                                            |
| ------ | ------------------------------------------ |
|        | I                                          |
| keep   | watch on my earthly                        |
| keep   | -sakes while sipping from my               |
| keep   | cup.                                       |
|        | I                                          |
| keep   | my whole body to the grindstone,           |
| keep   | 2 eyes on my bottom line like a book-      |
| keep   | -er.                                       |
|        | I                                          |
| keep   | fit at night on a gym bike,                |
| keep   | abreast of news through tweeters who       |
| keep   | on tweeting and retweeting.                |
|        | I                                          |
| keep   | time on my latest device,                  |
| keep   | losing touch with natural history.         |
| 'Keep  | this up,'                                  |
|        | I                                          |
| keep   | thinking, 'and you'll                      |
| keep   | being mistaken for someone who             |
| keep   | -s trying to                               |
| keep   | up with the Trumps.'                       |
|        | I                                          |
| keep   | trying to                                  |
| keep   | my cool on this globe that                 |
| keep   | -s warming, resisting by                   |
| keep   | -ing down my carbon footprint.             |
|        | I                                          |
|        | cannot                                     |
| keep   | up with this sci-fi future.                |

# Sylvan Sightings

At Beaufort Lake,
a holidaymaker sights
a bashful billed bunyip
surfacing from its aquatic abode
to study the local terrestrial

fauna.
Near Wedderburn,
a farmer has seen a flying saucer
descend to a field of failing wheat crops
and flatten them into a pattern
resembling the face of David

Bowie.
In inner Bendigo,
a visiting theatre critic
has favourably reviewed the operatics
of Dame Nellie Melba's ghost
during a long night at the Hotel

Shamrock.
In the heart of Ballarat,
the statue of poet Robert Burns
has repositioned itself overnight,
breaking the written laws of physics
to pet its ever-loyal Scottish

sheepdog.
On the streets of Maryborough,
a senior secondary chemistry
teacher's rare discovery
of a 23-carat gold nugget
has been ascribed to Alexandrian

alchemy.
All across the Victorian
Goldfields, journos
are patiently
waiting
to run with
long-awaited news
of a second gold

rush.

# Back to the Sea

The Australian
summer burns out as we march into
autumnal climes. Landlocked here in Central Victoria,
I take a short walk around a shallow reservoir. I then pack my
jet black sedan for a road trip to Torquay to catch one final stream
of curvaceous, salty waves direct from Bass Strait. When I finally arrive

oceanside, I pull up and sigh at the sight       of those oceanic waves
rhythmically rippling, rising, rolling, and      ramming into wet sand.
The roiling of that water as it's sucked back      out to sea calls to me
with the most melodious urgency. I speedily      get out of my jet
black car with a foamy surfboard made to ride      waves.

Clad from neck to ankle in neoprene, I sprint bare
-foot through baked sand to the sound, sight, and scent
of salt water rhythmically rippling, rising, rolling, ramming,
and roiling. My senses urge my legs to move ever onward—back
to the only place where nature can elevate me from the monotony of life.

# Terra Australis Breath

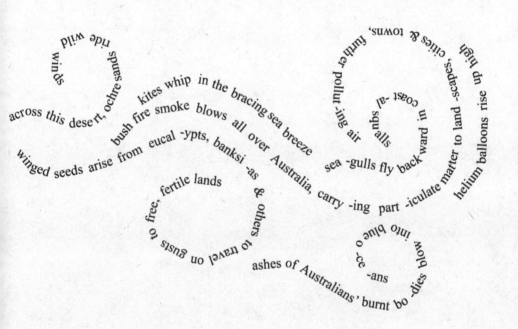

ride wild winds across this desert, ochre sands winged seeds arise from eucal -ypts, banksi -as & others to travel on gusts to free, fertile lands kites whip in the bracing sea breeze bush fire smoke blows all over Australia, carry -ing part -iculate matter to land -scapes, cities & towns, further pollut -ing air sea -gulls fly back -ward in coast -al squalls helium balloons rise up high blow into blue o- -ce -ans ashes of Australians' burnt bo- -dies

# PART TWO
# THE BIOPSYCHOSOCIAL MODEL

# The Palm of My Left Hand

*Dja Dja Wurrung Country, 1991*

**i.**
poolside, i slip
        & fall—my palm
opens to metal

**ii.**
blood stains my hand—
              i will this skin opening
to close & contain

**iii.**
schoolyard at recess—
i keep hands in pockets
to hide my bandage

**iv.**
the doc unwraps
        my wound then—while checking
—reopens flesh

**v.**
i stretch out my palm—
           a new scar transects
the head & heart lines

# Frida Kahlo's Backbone

*After her painting* The Broken Column *(1944)*

Frida Kahlo was born in July 1907
    in old Coyoacán, Mexico.
She was six years old going on 47
    when polio struck her down.
She survived with a shrivelled leg
    and threw herself into sports.
Proud parents stoked the bright fire
    of young Frida's quick mind.
At 18, Frida was in a motor crash
    that fractured her to pieces.
Though she was lucky to be alive,
    her life goals burned to ash.
Frida went from aspiring doctor to
    patient trapped in body casts.
She was alone, in pain and unable
    to ambulate for near a year.
She began to create oil paintings
    that mirrored her pained life.
Diego Rivera loved her portraits
    of her own body and mind.
They became a married couple—
    old painter & new painter.
Frida suffered a miscarriage then
    painted her beloved fetus.
In her art, she birthed herself into
    a bloodstained landscape.
The resilient love between Diego
    & Frida was often tested.
Diego's affair with Frida's sister
    made Frida crop her hair.
Frida divided into two Fridas with
    the power of self-nurture.

She processed her darkest memories
while soaking in bathwater.
She offset the darkness with vibrant
strokes of colour & humour.
Her art was exhibited and praised in
Mexico, the US and Europe.
Picasso praised her art and gave her
gold, hand-shaped earrings.
Frida connected with art lovers who
felt her loneliness and pain.
She had many orthopaedic surgeries,
only to continue suffering.
She painted a still life of watermelon
pieces as the end closed in.
Frida Kahlo left her body in July 1954
in old Coyoacán, Mexico.

# Clouds

You spent most your life
with your head in the clouds
of smoke that billowed forth
from the O-shaped mouths
of the ones you love.

You never smoked
so much as one cigarette
in all your cloudy days
spent in places you came
to call bittersweet home.

Your parents and husband
fought for breath and coughed
blood before dying one by one,
leaving you and your
dear daughter all alone.

You lived on as a widow
who sold bright bouquets to
people who knew you
by a smoker's cough, a cheeky smile,
and photos of your granddaughter.

When the time came for you
to fight for breath and cough blood,
you felt a poignant love
for the grand one who shaved
her tiny head for your cure.

The chemo made you
bald like your granddaughter
and vomit like your daughter
yet kept you alive
for the birth of your grandson.

All winter, your oncologist
wore the crochet scarf
that you made especially for her
just before moving out
of your bittersweet home.

Your family often visited
your spacious hospice room
to be there with you
as you faded like the old
flowers in your closed shop.

You spent your last days
with your head in the clouds
of soothing words that flowed forth
from the inverting, U-shaped mouths
of the ones you love.

# The Pharmacokinetics of Paracetamol

A paracetamol tablet

won't hurt

you; it will alleviate

your aches.

That white tablet'll

move down

your GIT and swiftly

disintegrate.

Within an hour, it'll

virtually all

be absorbed into the

bloodstream.

The [paracetamol]-

time plot

will

reach its max

then

drop by half-

lives.

The area under

the

curve will

then

capture the drug's

kinetics.

Particles will've gone

through fine

branches straight into

most tissues.

This paracetamol

won't hurt

you; it will alleviate

your aches.

It will metabolise

in your liver

to produce inactive

metabolites.

The chemicals will

move between

two compartments:

blood & urine.

The [metabolite]-

time plot

will

reach its max

then

drop by half-

lives.

The area under

the

curve will

then

capture metabolic

kinetics.

Within a day, it'll

virtually all

be excreted via the

urinary tract.

There will be nary

a trace of the

paracetamol left in

your system.

Your pain will have

become

distant—

a memory.

# An Abbreviated Case Study
# in Geriatric Orthopaedics

| | |
|---|---|
| The MD came in and spoke of | |
| a cheery older lady from the | ER |
| with a severely fractured | NOF |
| that would require a | THR. |
| The patient had a low | BMD |
| that could be explained by an | ADR |
| to a steroid taken orally | bd |
| before her fall and trip to the | ER. |
| She was on a benzo and a | TCA |
| that was being switched to an | SSRI. |
| She took meds for HT and a | CVA |
| as well as a long-term | PPI. |
| Notes written last month by an | RN |
| stated dependence in most | IADLs. |
| She was given IV morphine and | TPN |
| as she grew more dependent in | ADLs. |
| She said she felt like an actress on a | TV |
| show that made her cry yet | LOL. |
| She was a lively inpatient on *House* | *MD* |
| who yearned to get up and go | AWOL. |
| She had complications post | THR |
| and was hooked up to an | ECG. |
| Warfarin dosed according to | INR |
| was used to prevent a | DVT. |
| She looked like she'd been in an | MVA, |
| all scratched and bruised there in the | ICU. |
| Her medical record said | 'NKA'. |
| The look in her deep-set eyes said | 'IOU'. |

# The Second Type

*Declare the past, diagnose the present, foretell the future…*
—*Hippocrates,* Epidemics I *(circa 400 BC)*

Your body is a picture of health
in all respects except hormonally.
Something is not quite right
in that curved archipelago
of your pancreas.

From your islets of Langerhans,
that peptide hormone known as
insulin

                                                   swims out

into red seas
decreasingly frequently,
only to meet staunch resistance
to the regulation of blood sugar levels.

Your blood sugar rises
and falls
amid relentless waves.

This is why
you harbour a thirst, a hunger, an urge
and more besides.

You ask me why
this is happening to you
at age 32.

Based on our discussion, I give you 3 reasons:

1.  your family history of type 2 diabetes
2.  that fast food you eat
3.  your sedentary lifestyle.

You ask me what
you can do to manage this problem
besides taking metformin.

Based on the literature, I offer you 2 options:

1.  take the time to eat better
2.  exercise every day of your life.

I hand you a booklet while you stare at me
through vision that may soon turn blurry
if we don't manage this problem.

Eventually, you manage
a polite nod
and slowly get up to leave
in silence.

# This Morning Routine

still
no light
shines here—
no photons
enter half-
open eyes
for hours on end

till
low light
creeps round
the sides of curtains
to the same old sound
of an alarm tune
that continues

till
feet move
to the kitchen
and hands hold
a dirty kettle
below
a running tap

still
water
molecules vibrate
while the aroma
of instant coffee
crystals

fills
nostrils
and half–
light filters
thru open shut
-ters into half–
closed eyes

# Assisted Living & Dying

*I love roles that, like I said before, are challenging and risky…*
—*Caroline Dhavernas,* Flickering Myth *(2017)*

Certain viewers
would perceive
poignant beauty
across cult Canadian actress
Caroline Dhavernas'
body of
work

,

particularly her noughties role
in *W o n d e r f a l l s*
as a retail clerk & philosopher
who (un)willingly helps
struggling strangers
live full lives

juxtaposed with her new role
in *Mary Kills People*
as an ER doctor & counsellor
who (un)willingly helps
d y i n g  patients
die.

# Poly Days

eating polyunsaturated

                            fats in hot food

drinking polysaccharide

                            sugars in hot drinks

reusing a polystyrene

                            cup at driver reviver stops

studying polypharmacy

                            in my pharmacy

                                            degrees

studying polymer

                    chemistry

                            just for funsies

analysing polychotomous

                                variables rather

                                        than dichotomies

                  trying to be a polymath

              applying a polygraph

abstaining from polygamy

              getting over polymorphisms

                  watching Polly & colleagues

                                    from *Fawlty Towers*

                                              on VHS

# Life (P)review

*May 2005*

I cannot remember
the message in the captain's words,
only their infectious trepidation.

Suddenly, we
drop.
The fearful silence…
punctured by a scream of terror.

My plane window
becomes a porthole
with a cloudy view of the sea
metres below.

The short life
that flashes before me
is not the one spent
on *that* island nation—
Australia—
but, rather, a parallel life
growing up
on *this* island nation—
Malta.

I am walking
hand in hand with my mother
along crumbly white cliffs
that soar steeply over azure waters,
headed for St Mary Magdalene's
lonely stone chapel.

I am following
in the footsteps of my father
through the serried crowds
of the Marsaxlokk fish market,
my senses flooded
with colour & odour.

I am running
with my best friends
through the megalithic stone ruins
of Ħaġar Qim
during the best school excursion
I can recall.

I am writing
amid spectacular architecture
at an outdoor café in Valletta
about the monochrome medieval
history of the Knights
Hospitaller.

I am entering
the old, walled capital—
Mdina—through its imposing,
lion-guarded gate
during a fleeting field trip
for my history degree.

I am peering
up at the enormous dome
of Mosta Basilica,
wondering
what manner of complex physics
allowed a Luftwaffe bomb to crash
land
amid an unsuspecting congregation
but not explode.

I am listening
to the thunderous applause
of fellow air travellers
aboard a passenger plane
recently landed on a runway
at Malta International Airport.

# Return to Realism

*Regional Victoria, February 2020*

I drive into the heart
of the storm
to see you
in person
on just another Day

of Saturn.
Everything & everyone
other than you in this satiny milieu
is a distraction
from what actually matters

to me.
As rain falls on my vehicle,
I resolve
to never
compare you to
anything or anyone
other than you
unless you ask me to

in person.
As I pull up
at your rural residence,
I see myself
pulling up a seat across from you
at your wooden kitchen table

and forgetting
everything & everyone
other than you
to the sound of the storm
outside.

# Alternative Meanings of COVID-19

COronaVIrus Disease 19
Cancel Overseas traVel ImmeDiately 19...
COnsider Viable alternatIves to hanDshakes 19...
Cough/sneeze On the V of the epIconDyle 19...
Clean dOwn Virally Infected Desks 19...
Call Off Various Important Dates 19...
Close dOwn Virtually everythIng Downtown 19...
Create an Optimal Vaccine rapIDly 19...
Chill Out/Vegetate InDoors 19...
COmfort ourselVes wIth Distractions 19...
Come Over Very Infrequently, Dear 19...
COmmunicate Via the Internet insteaD 19...
Combine Our Voices In soliDarity 19...
Care fOr the Vulnerable In this worlD 19...
COntain this VIral spreaD 19...

| W | F | H |
|---|---|---|
| Worked | From | Home |
| Washed | Filthy | Hands |
| Weathered | Free-to-air | Horrors |
| Wandered | From | Happiness |
| Worried | For | Humanity |
| Waited | For | Horsemen |
| Woke | From | Haze |
| Whistled | For | Hours |
| Wandered | Four-walled | Habitat |
| Welcomed | Forgotten | Hobbies |
| Web-searched | Family | History |
| Wished | For | Health |

# iso

*after Mari B-Li Donni's installation* Isolation: The Fine Line *(2020)*

sea

        -ted

 a-

     lone

here

   not

                       over    there

           sudden

sep

     -aration

        deso

-lation

   iso

-lation

 on an i

      -sland

     O  so

       cut

  off

  mask

     off

     model's

       legs

crossed

        mind                      elsewhere

fresh-cut

       red        flo - wers

 tardy
eggless
Easter
Bunny

by   an

        un-

marked

          grave

    blue

  butter
     -fly

at    rest
  on
    a match

-ing

     blue

  tissue
    bo
-x

no

.1

else

around

no

1

2      talk      2

BUT

still some-

1                    who

some    -    times

calls      U

&

asks

U

R

U

OK      ?

# These Sources of Solace

*... I really do hope that I'm helping people...*
*—Fiona Apple, NPR (2020)*

*Regional Victoria, December 2020*

The trough is
                stable
                                on our epi curve.
                                I'm sat at the
                table
eating porridge
with pieces of
                apple
                                while listening
                                to alt-pop
                staples
from the new
LP by Fiona
                Apple:
                                one of the precious
                                few pleasur-
                able
things to have
come from a de-
                bacle
                                of a calendar year.

# Corona-gram Distillation

co ro na vi rus
carnivorous
rancorous
saviour
cursor
virus
ruin
air
us
i

# The Pain of Distance & Time

*In loving memory of Lily (1923-2012) & Eric (1927-2016) Wheeler*
*Adelaide, South Australia, 2012 & Bendigo, Victoria, 2016*

| | |
|---|---|
| Once | Once |
| there was | there was |
| a lioness | a songbird |
| of a lady | of a larrikin |
| who spent | who spent |
| her childhood | his childhood |
| & adulthood | & adulthood |
| in the company | in the company |
| of antique dolls | of audiences |
| & teddy bears | & customers |
| that she vigilantly | who intently |
| watched | listened |
| over till | to him till |
| the midwinter day | the midwinter day |
| she died. | he died. |
| I was far away | I was close by |
| —interstate— | —at his bedside— |
| when her selfless | when his selfless |
| love for family | love for family |
| passed | passed |
| into history | into history |
| to the painful | to the painful |
| maternal sound | surreal sight |
| of my dear mother | of my mother's father |
| trying | lying |
| valiantly | supine |
| to get | with mouth |
| words out | open, |
| between | frozen in |
| sobs. | song. |
| I will sorely miss | I will sorely miss |
| the doll doctor | the country singer |

&
till
the midwinter
day
I die.

# Maternal Memories

*In loving memory of Judy Leach (1953-2020)*

### i.

Mum,
you've
a l w a y s
been the heart
of this close-knit clan.
You wisely lead, fiercely defend,
generously give, wholly love. You've gone well above
and far beyond to make us three children and our dear Dad feel as special as royals.
You're a skilled antique dealer and natural teacher—
you taught us how to live life right.
Your strong spirit lights
paths forwards
& soothes
pained
hearts.

### ii.

We state
the sweet simple things
you yearned to do
on your ICU deathbed:
to return home
& keep cooking meals
for others;
to go out
in your new second-hand car
& buy bargain-priced antiques
at op shops.
As we speak about you,

your song comes on
the car radio: 'Over the Rainbow'
by your namesake.

Judy's angelic vocals
coupled with the                    soaring
instrumental arrangement
strike major chords
& render us
speechless.

I recall how you adored
this sweet simple song
we haven't heard
in so                               long,
how the funeral
director mistakenly played
that cover version you abhorred

at your burial.

During this rare moment
with my baby sister,
I look her in the face—
lacrimal secretions
in familiar eyes
reflect mine
as we draw ever closer
to our final destination.

Here I am—
an off-duty statistician—
wholeheartedly believing
in the beautiful spirituality
of synchronicity.

| | |
|---|---|
| Everything changed<br>near the beginning<br>of this dire decade. | Everything changed<br>near the beginning<br>of this dire decade. |
| Most notably & excruciatingly,<br>I lost my beloved Mum | There was an addition to my family:<br>I picked up a cavoodle pup |
| between the 1st & 2nd<br>waves<br>of COVID-19 here in Victoria, Australia. | between the 1st & 2nd<br>waves<br>of COVID-19 here in Victoria, Australia. |
| Her unconditional love<br>now lives on in artefacts, fond memories<br>& her spiritual gaze. | His unconditional love<br>now manifests in tail wags, frenetic licks<br>& a knowing gaze. |
| Her unconditional love<br>sustains. | His unconditional love<br>sustains. |

hairs found in hair ties: strands of her hair

DNA; traces of her tidy head of hair

# Notes

'**This Place of Birth**' is a haiku sequence about my birthplace of Bendigo—a regional Victorian gold rush town situated on the unceded lands of the Dja Dja Wurrung people. The nature reserve mentioned here is the one closest to my home, namely the Grassy Flat Reservoir Bushland Reserve in Kennington. I changed my first tyre on the first day of Victoria's fourth lockdown: Friday 28 May 2021. My mother is buried beneath gumtrees at Bendigo Monumental Cemetery. When writing this haiku sequence, I drew inspiration from the following article:

> Bullock, O. (2021). Haiku for recovery: An immersive workshop. *TEXT: Journal of Writing and Writing Courses*, 25(1): 1-26.

Bullock's essay taught me that it is acceptable to write four-line haiku with visual elements.

'**This Contemporary Palette**' is a fictional sestina exploring a couple's relationships with six colours or shades: vantablack, beige, neo mint, dragon's blood, electric blue, and heliotrope. This poem was inspired by a reference book entitled *The Secret Lives of Colour* (Kassia St Clair, John Murray, 2016) as well as the HBO television series *Game of Thrones* (2011-2019). 'VANTAs' stands for 'vertically aligned carbon nanotube arrays'—the technology used to create vantablack. In the penultimate stanza, 'Electric Blue' refers to a song from Australian band Icehouse's LP *Man of Colours* (1987).

'**Bioluminescence**': The crystal jelly (*Aequorea victoria*) is a bioluminescent jellyfish. Members of this species are described as 'bioluminescent' because they naturally give of light. 'Bloom' is a collective noun for jellyfish.

'**Symbological Statement**' addresses the idea of post-truth logic. The mathematical symbols used throughout this poem are defined as follows:

> - 'IF' and 'THEN' form part of conditional (IF-THEN) statements used in computer programming.
>
> - '$\Sigma$' means 'sum'. It can be read here as 'some', giving 'someone' in line 2 and 'something' in lines 11 and 15.
>
> - $\sqrt{}$ is the symbol for 'square root'.
>
> - $\infty$ means 'infinity'.
>
> - $\neq$ means 'does not equal'.
>
> - ? can be read here as 'question'.

- π is the mathematical symbol for the number pi. It can be read here as 'pie'.

- ÷ can be read here as 'divide'.

- ∫ means 'integral'.

- Δ is a symbol for uncertainty. It can be read here as 'uncertain'.

- x can be read here as 'times'.

- ¬ means 'not'.

- OR is a Boolean logical operator used in computer programming.

Towards the end of the poem, '1984' and '2 + 2 = 4' refer to the mathematically incorrect phrase '2 + 2 = 5' from George Orwell's novel *Nineteen Eighty-Four* (Secker & Warburg, 1949).

'N of 1': A photon is a particle of light. A Möbius strip is a one-sided band or loop that, in many scientific illustrations, features undulations.

'Fractional' is an ekphrastic poem based on Mari B-Li Donni's digital photograph of the same name. Mari passed away in March 2022—nine months after I wrote this poem. Empedocles (circa 494 BC–circa 434 BC) was a Greek philosopher who defined the four classical elements: water, earth, air, and fire.

'(Un)real' is an ekphrastic poem inspired by a *Visual Verse* image attributed to Mae Mu (https://visualverse.org/images/mae-mu/). From ancient times up until the 19th century, the term 'natural philosophy' referred to the philosophical study of nature and the Universe. Natural philosophy led to natural science—a contemporary branch of science encompassing the physical sciences and the life sciences.

'Atmospheric' is a science fiction piece describing how it might feel to free fall through the planet Jupiter—a gas giant without a clear-cut solid surface. This prose poem was inspired by a scientific illustration of Jupiter's atmospheric layers and corresponding altitudes and pressures (https://pages.uoregon.edu/jimbrau/BrauImNew/Chap11/7th/AT_7e_Figure_11_07.jpg). The 'stratosphere', 'haze layer', and 'troposphere' are the three outermost layers of Jupiter's atmosphere. A 'thought experiment' involves thinking through the practical consequences and implications of a given theory or hypothesis. 'Albert' refers to Albert Einstein (1879-1955) while 'Katie' refers to Katie Bouman (1989-), whose computer imagery work led to the first ever image of a black hole. Katie's black hole image corroborates Albert's theory of relativity.

'Radio-luminous': In the opening stanza of this poem, 'so(u)l' indicates both the English word 'soul' and the Latin word 'sol', which means 'sun'. A photon is a particle of light. The 'Aurora Australis' is otherwise known as the 'Southern Lights'. A 'Duchenne smile' is a genuine one involving both the mouth and the eyes.

'**My Peace Lily**' was inspired by a digital photograph of my peace lily plant.

'**My Harlequin**': The shape and content of this visual poem were inspired by a digital photograph of my first adopted pet—a Magpie Harlequin Rabbit. The poem references various scientific facts about the Magpie Harlequin Rabbit.

'**West-East**' was inspired by a reference book entitled *Shrubs and Trees for Australian Gardens* (Ernest E. Lord and J.H. Willis, Lothian Publishing Company Pty Ltd, 1982). The plant species named in the left-hand and right-hand columns are native to the west and east coasts of Australia, respectively. The stanza 'A rosy / Sydney rose / responding to its / botanical name—*Boronia / serrulate*—is just as sweet / and dramatically more / taxonomic.' refers to the famous line about a sweet-smelling rose from William Shakespeare's 1597 play *Romeo and Juliet*. The red-and-green kangaroo paw (*Anigozanthos manglesii*) and New South Wales waratah (*Telopea speciosissima*) are the floral emblems of Western Australia and New South Wales, respectively.

'**In Memory of an Island Species**' references a 2014 article published in *The Conversation* by John Woinarski, Don Driscoll, and Hal Cogger (https://theconversation.com/vale-gump-the-last-known-christmas-island-forest-skink-30252). In the field of zoology, an 'endling' is the last surviving member of a given species.

'**The Australian Anthropo-seen**' describes the impacts of climate change on a threatened Australian animal: the koala. This poem contains details sourced from a 2009 scientific report by Chris Johnson, Jane DeGabriel, and Ben Moore (https://www.iucn.org/sites/dev/files/import/downloads/fact_sheet_red_list_koala_v2.pdf).

The piece's koala-shaped appearance gives rise to a visual effect outlined by French philosopher Michel Foucault in his book *This is Not a Pipe* (University of California Press, 1983, pages 24-25): words of poetry disappear when one views a visual poem's whole shape, while a visual poem's whole shape disappears when one reads the words. When one reads about the impacts of climate change on the koala, the koala disappears.

'**Summer Air**' describes the catastrophic 2019-20 Australian Bushfire Season from the perspectives of two people. One of these people (Rachel Rayner) lives in Sydney on unceded Dharug Country while the other (myself) lives in regional Victoria on unceded Dja Dja Wurrung Country.

**'Sylvan Sightings'** is a fictional poem featuring real-world references. Beaufort, Wedderburn, Bendigo, Ballarat, and Maryborough are all located within the Victorian Goldfields in south-eastern Australia. The bunyip is a mythological creature believed to have inhabited bodies of freshwater throughout Australia. David Bowie (1947-2016) was an English singer-songwriter who often wrote about space and became one of the most famous singers of his generation. Dame Nellie Melba (1861-1931) was a Melbourne-born operatic soprano who performed internationally and became one of the most famous singers of her generation. Melba stayed in the Shamrock Hotel, Bendigo during the Edwardian Era. Ballarat's statue of Scottish poet Robert Burns (1759-1796) was unveiled in 1887, becoming Australia's first statue dedicated to a poet. The last working gold mine in Maryborough (the largest city in the Central Goldfields Shire) closed during 1918. The Victorian Gold Rush began in the early 1850s and ended in the late 1860s.

**'Back to the Sea':** Bass Strait is the narrow stretch of water separating Tasmania from mainland Australia. The word 'neoprene' refers to synthetic rubbers from which wetsuits are made.

**'Terra Australis Breath':** 'Terra Australis' is Latin for 'Southern Land'. The contemporary name for the continent and country of Australia was derived from 'Terra Australis'.

**'The Palm of My Left Hand':** The head and heart lines are the two topmost lines running across the palm of the human hand. In the pseudoscience of palmistry, the 'head line' is said to reveal an individual's thinking processes while the 'heart line' is said to reveal an individual's emotional capacity. On some people's palms, the head and heart lines are divided by a so-called 'fate line', which is said to show the extent to which one's life is governed by fate. While I don't have a natural fate line, I do have a scar in a similar location.

**'Frida Kahlo's Backbone':** This vertebrae-shaped poem reflects my belief that the life of Frida Kahlo (1907-1954) embodies the interdisciplinary fields of health humanities and arts in health. The poem's shape and content were informed by Frida Kahlo's painting *The Broken Column* (1944) and Hayden Herrera's *Frida: A Biography of Frida Kahlo* (Perennial, 1983).

**'Clouds'** seeks to communicate the risks of passive smoking as well as a fictional patient's experience of living and dying with lung cancer. This poem was inspired by my time working in hospital settings as well as the 2016 edition of Cancer Council Victoria's *Optimal Care Pathway for People with Lung Cancer*. This document addresses the whole patient journey undertaken by people with lung cancer, from prevention and early detection through to end-of-life care.

'The Pharmacokinetics of Paracetamol' is an exercise in visual science communication. The poem's content is based on knowledge gained while completing my pharmacy degree at La Trobe University, Bendigo. The acronmyn 'GIT' stands for 'gastrointestinal tract'. The square brackets in '[paracetamol]- / time plot' and '[metabolite]- / time plot' mean 'concentration', giving 'paracetamol concentration- / time plot' and 'metabolite concentration- / time plot', respectively. The poem's shape is based on a graph published in the following research paper:

de Martino, M. & Chiarugi, A. (2015). Recent advances in pediatric use of oral paracetamol in fever and pain management. *Pain and Therapy*, 4(2): 149-168.

'An Abbreviated Case Study in Geriatric Orthopaedics' was informed by my university studies and experience working in hospital settings. The poem refers to the Fox television series *House MD* (2004-2012). The jagged line formed by the abbreviations is intended to represent a hip fracture. Here is a glossary of abbreviations (listed in order of appearance in the poem):

MD – medical doctor

ER – emergency room

NOF – neck of femur (i.e. a part of the hip)

THR – total hip replacement

BMD – bone mineral density

ADR – adverse drug reaction

bd – twice daily

benzo – benzodiazepine

TCA – tricyclic antidepressant

SSRI – selective serotonin reuptake inhibitor

HT – hypertension

CVA – cerebrovascular accident (i.e. stroke)

PPI – proton pump inhibitor

RN – registered nurse

IADLs – instrumental activities of daily living

IV – intravenous

TPN – total parenteral nutrition

ADLs – activities of daily living

TV – television

LOL – laugh out loud

MD – medical doctor

AWOL – absent without official leave

THR – total hip replacement

ECG – electrocardiogram

INR – international normalised ratio

DVT – deep vein thrombosis

MVA – motor vehicle accident

ICU – intensive care unit

NKA – no known allergies

IOU – I owe you.

'The Second Type': The title of this poem refers to type 2 diabetes mellitus (T2DM)—a chronic metabolic disorder caused by genetic and lifestyle factors. The 'islets of Langerhans' are groups of cells in the pancreas that secrete the hormone insulin, which regulates blood sugar (i.e. glucose) levels. The islets of Langerhans were named after German pathologist and physiologist Paul Langerhans (1847-1888), who discovered the islets in Berlin during 1869. Metformin is a biguanide medication used to control blood glucose levels in those living with T2DM.

'This Morning Routine': A photon is a particle of light.

'Assisted Living & Dying' refers to two North American television series: *Wonderfalls* (Fox, 2004) and *Mary Kills People* (Global, 2017-2019). Montreal-based actress Caroline Dhavernas had the lead role in both series. This poem addresses the ethics of intervening in people's lives and providing voluntary assisted dying services.

'Poly Days' mentions hotel maid and waitress Polly Sherman—a fictional character from the BBC2 television series *Fawlty Towers* (1975-1979).

'Life (P)review': I wrote this poem upon viewing a prompt, specifically a *Visual Verse* image by Rude Ltd (https://visualverse.org/images/rude/). This poem blends the real-life story of my perilous flight from Italy to Malta with a set of fictional flashbacks to a youth spent in the Maltese Archipelago. The flashbacks describe places I visited upon safely landing in Malta. Regarding the poem's title, a 'life review' is an understudied phenomenon whereby a near-death experience triggers montage-like flashbacks to moments across an individual's lifespan.

**'Return to Realism':** 'Day / of Saturn' refers to the etymology of the word 'Saturday'. Both the day of the week 'Saturday' and the planet 'Saturn' were named after the deity 'Saturn'—the ancient Roman god of, among other matters, agriculture and liberation.

**'Alternative Meanings of COVID-19':** This poem aims to communicate public health decisions and messages related to the COVID-19 pandemic. The 'epicondyle' refers to bones in the elbow.

**'These Sources of Solace':** The term 'epi curve' is short for 'epidemiological curve'—a type of graph visualising the number of cases of a disease, such as COVID-19, over time. In this context, a 'trough' is the lowest case count on the epi curve relative to higher counts in the past and future. The poem's undulating shape represents waves of the ongoing COVID-19 pandemic as well as upcoming pandemics. In this poem, 'alt-pop / staples' refers to songs such as 'Under the Table' and 'Shameika' from Fiona Apple's LP *Fetch the Bolt Cutters* (2020). This LP received the highest ever *Metacritic* Metascore (98%), topped numerous end-of-year lists, and won the 2021 Grammy Award for Best Alternative Music Album. It has been a source of solace for listeners during particularly difficult times.

**'Corona-gram Distillation':** Each line of this poem contains only letters from the word 'coronavirus'. While the word 'carnivorous' is a perfect anagram of 'coronavirus', the words that follow feature progressively fewer letters from the source word. The poem gradually distils down to the word 'i'.

**'The Pain of Distance & Time':** My maternal grandmother, Lily Wheeler (1923-2012), was a lifelong doll collector and repairer. During the 1970s, she moved from Melbourne to Bendigo with my grandfather and young mother so as to open the Antique Doll & Toy Museum of Bendigo and the Bendigo Doll Hospital. They remained in Bendigo for the rest of their lives. Mum met my father while working at the Southern Cross TV8 network in Bendigo and, ultimately, followed in her mother's footsteps by becoming an antique dealer. My maternal grandfather, Eric Wheeler (1927-2016), was a salesperson as well as a guitarist and country singer. He released multiple records and regularly performed at live events. I lived in Adelaide at the time my grandmother passed and in Bendigo at the time my grandfather passed. The right-hand column of this poem complements a prose piece that I published during 2016 alongside a digital photograph in *Pulse—voices from the heart of medicine* (https://pulsevoices. org/index.php/visuals/the-day-grandpa-passed).

'**Maternal Memories i.**' is a Fibonacci poem whereby each line's syllable count aligns with the first 8 numbers in the naturally occurring Fibonacci sequence (1, 1, 2, 3, 5, 8, 13, and 21). I wrote this poem two days after my mother unexpectedly passed away on 6 June 2020. If I had the chance to say some final words to Mum, these are the words I would say.

'**Maternal Memories ii.**' was inspired by my late mother's favourite song: the original version of 'Over the Rainbow' from the 1939 film *The Wizard of Oz*. This Academy Award-winning song was composed by Harold Arlen. The lyrics were written by E.Y. Harburg and sung by Judy Garland. The acronym 'ICU' stands for 'intensive care unit'.

'**Maternal Memories iii.**': Mum's artefacts include life symbols displayed at her funeral: a framed family photograph, various stage show programs, her favourite novel (*Where the Crawdads Sing* by Delia Owen), a perfume bottle, a Royal Winton teapot, and a toy koala from her childhood. Mum kept the toy koala at her side all her life. On the eve of Melbourne's second lockdown, I travelled from Bendigo to Melbourne to pick up a new addition to my family—a cavoodle pup I named Rollo.

'**Maternal Memories iv.**': DNA (deoxyribonucleic acid) is a molecule comprising two helical strands of hereditary material—the genetic instructions for life.

# Acknowledgements

I am over the Sun about publishing a full-length collection of poems with Recent Work Press! From the moment I purchased my first stack of Recent Work Press titles at the Poetry on Move Festival 2019, I knew that I wanted to publish with this innovative, poetry-focused publisher. I am grateful to the indefatigable Shane Strange for all the guidance, advice, patience, and collegiality. Shane, many thanks for seeing potential in my poetry and for taking the time to help me sculpt *Natural Philosophies*. You have enabled me to find and transmit my voice.

I have many more people to thank. A huge thank you to my science poetry buddy, poet and science communicator Rachel Rayner, for the unswerving inspiration, encouragement, and feedback as well as the fruitful collaborative work on 'Summer Air'. Rachel, the poems in this collection wouldn't exist if it weren't for you. I am indebted to the amazing Alicia Sometimes and those who participated in the Writing NSW workshop *Online Feedback: Poetry with Alicia Sometimes* (15/07/2019-29/11/2019). Alicia and fellow workshop participants provided generous feedback on my poetry, helping me to develop some of the poems featured in *Natural Philosophies*. I would also like to thank Leah Kaminsky for publishing my first ever poem and Tina Giannoukos for editing my debut book—the chapbook *Chronicity* (Melbourne Poets Union, 2020). Leah and Tina, you made me believe that I could one day become an established poet. In terms of people here in regional Victoria, my thanks to the Write Stuff Bendigo collective, Bendigo Writers Council, and co-workers at Monash University School of Rural Health for supporting my poetry. I say a prayer of thanks for the generosity and collegiality of Axedale-based artist Mari B-Li Donni. In the final years of her life, Mari created and shared the thought-provoking, moving artworks that inspired the ekphrastic poems 'Fractional' and 'iso'. I am deeply, deeply thankful to my dear family—both those who are living and those who have passed on—for all the love, support, and memories.

I acknowledge the hard-working editorial staff and curators who published or exhibited many of the poems from *Natural Philosophies* (some in earlier forms or with different titles) across the following journals, magazines, books, or exhibitions:

*Verandah, Black Bough Poetry, Meniscus Literary Journal, Chronicity* (Melbourne Poets Union, 2020), *Live Encounters, Unusual Work, The Mathematical Intelligencer, Co.Lab Exhibition 2021* (Creative Communities, City of Greater Bendigo), *Visual Verse, AntipodeanSF, New Shoots Garden of Poems* (Red Room Company), *Rabbit: a journal for nonfiction poetry, Plumwood Mountain, Jalmurra, NatureVolve,*

*What I Did Last Week: Online Exhibition* (Creative Communities, City of Greater Bendigo), *Poetry for the Planet: An Anthology of Imagined Futures* (Litoria Press, 2021), *Featured Artist of the Month* gallery (Emporium Creative Hub), *Science Write Now, Blue Bottle Journal, Otoliths, No News: 90 Poets Reflect on a Unique BBC Newscast* (Recent Work Press, 2020), *The Journal of Humanities in Rehabilitation, Medical Humanities, Cordite Poetry Review, Still You: Poems of Illness and Healing* (Wolf Ridge Press, 2020), *Journal of Art and Aesthetics in Nursing and Health Sciences, International Journal of Disease Reversal and Prevention, Mindshare, The Blue Nib, Red Wolf Journal, The Galway Review, Life in Lockdown Exhibition* (Goldfields Libraries), *Poetry and Covid, Stereo Stories,* and *Burrow.*

# About the Author

**Michael J. Leach** is an academic and poet with passionate interests in health humanities and science communication. He has a set of scientific tertiary qualifications: a Bachelor of Pharmacy, Graduate Certificate of Science (Applied Statistics), Master of Biostatistics, and Doctor of Philosophy (PhD) in Pharmacoepidemiology. Upon completing his PhD project at the University of South Australia, Michael boxed up his books and returned to his birthplace of Bendigo—a regional Victorian city located on the unceded lands of the Dja Dja Wurrung people. Michael now undertakes interdisciplinary research and teaching at the Monash University School of Rural Health, where he holds a senior lecturer position. Outside office hours, he pens poetry and plays. Michael's poems reside in *Rabbit, Cordite, Meniscus, Verandah, Consilience, The Sciku Project, NatureVolve, Plumwood Mountain, Medical Humanities*, the *Medical Journal of Australia*, and elsewhere. His poems have also been anthologised in *One Surviving Poem* (In Case of Emergency Press, 2019), *No News* (Recent Work Press, 2020), *Still You* (Wolf Ridge Press, 2020), *Poetry for the Planet* (Litoria Press, 2021), *Lockdown Poetry* (Liquid Amber Press, 2021), and *The 2021 Hippocrates Prize Anthology* (The Hippocrates Press, 2021). Michael's debut poetry collection—a chapbook entitled *Chronicity*—was published by Melbourne Poets Union in 2020. His science-themed plays *The Math* and *Astronomical Connection* were performed by Bendigo Theatre Company in 2019 and 2021, respectively.

www.ingramcontent.com/pod-product-compliance
Ingram Content Group Australia Pty Ltd
76 Discovery Rd, Dandenong South VIC 3175, AU
AUHW020721050325
407891AU00005B/34